THE
KINGDOM
OF GOD IS
AT HAND

THE KINGDOM OF GOD IS AT HAND

Compiled by Eugene Carvalho

The Kingdom of God is at Hand

To every human soul, with love…

TABLE OF CONTENTS

PURPOSE & ACKNOWLEDGEMENTS

The infallible Word of God for faith and conduct informs us that the Holy Spirit gives gifts to men and women of the Body of Christ. It states: "the gifts edify the body for the building up of the saints" (Eph. 4:12). I hope the talents and gifts the Lord has given me will be a blessing to someone else through the reading of this compilation.

I am grateful for the love from all family members, especially my parents Mary and Eugenio Carvalho. I am also grateful for the knowledge, wisdom and love of many pastors, teachers, professors and saints that the Lord has used to bless me. Lastly, I must not forget a special thank you to my dear friend Darrin Bouley for proofreading this material.

THE TWO KINGDOMS

I first and foremost want to give shouts of praise to the Lord for using me as an instrument to write another compilation, which will bless others for the glory of God. I just came from a Spanish restaurant called Taqueria El Zarape. While there, I ordered Tostada Con Pollo. That's a fried tortilla with refried beans, chicken, lettuce, tomato, provolone cheese, avocado, and cream cheese. It's a wonderful dish of food for five dollars, which is light, so the one hundred degree temperatures don't send you for a loop when you get outdoors...

I got halfway done eating my dinner and a beautiful young Mexican girl, about fourteen, came to my table selling candy apples. I explained to her I didn't eat them. I then started to explain to her regarding the kingdom of God and the kingdom of darkness. During my five minute sermon to her, I could see her eyes getting brighter and brighter from the anointing. I did not get into deep exegetical truths with her; I simply preached the Word. "For I am not ashamed of the gospel, for it is the power of God unto salvation to everyone who believes" (Ro. 1:16).[1]

It seems I eat many cold meals in restaurants because I'm spreading the "good

---

[1] All Scripture quotations, unless otherwise noted, are from the *New American Standard Bible*.

news" to the waiters and waitresses or individuals at the tables around me. She received Jesus as her Savior and then her younger brother came to the table. She got to hear the sermon twice. He also received the Lord, so now the living God dwells in them. Why did this all take place? Because the kingdom of God is at hand!

As I was driving out of the parking lot of that restaurant, the Lord informed me to start writing a book with that very title! *The Kingdom of God is at Hand...* I sowed and now I'm reaping. I got home and started typing the first paragraph and my telephone rang. The conversation reinforced the fact that we need to keep a real concrete perspective regarding the kingdom of God and the things present and the things to come.

Please allow me to explain. For about ten years, I have been mentoring individuals. Many have been alcoholics, drug addicts, and individuals just getting out of prison who need to be reformed back into society. So many times, the wives of these men are sick and tired of them passing out drunk, being dope sick and unresponsive. However, when the Lord transforms and restores them, their wives get sick and tired of them going to church three times a week. This particular gentleman explained to me this was the situation at his home.

I informed him on his way out the door to church tonight to notify his wife (who is unsaved) that it's not about watching television versus reading the Bible, staying awake or passing out, or going to church versus staying home. It's about, "Where are we going to spend eternity, in the kingdom of Heaven or in the kingdom of darkness?"

Kingdom of God / Kingdom of Heaven

"Terminology – According to all three Synoptics (which are the books of Matthew, Mark, and Luke) the kingdom of God was the central theme of the preaching and teaching of Jesus. Matthew substitutes "the kingdom of heaven" (lit. "the kingdom of the heavens)."

"The kingdom of God" is a rare expression in literature antedating our gospels. It does not occur in the Old Testament, although the idea is found throughout the Prophets, and it appears only a few times in intertestamental literature (references in Ladd, *Presence of the Future*, pp. 46, 130f.).

Scholars have differed about the basic meaning of the term, whether it conveys an "abstract" idea of God's rule or reign, or a "concrete" idea of God's rule over which He will reign—in this case, the age to come. It is established, however, that the meaning of the Hebrew *malkut*, which provides the historical background for Jesus' teaching, was the abstract idea of reign, rule. "They shall speak of the glory of thy kingdom and tell of thy power... Thy kingdom is an everlasting kingdom, and thy dominion endures throughout all generations" (Ps. 145:11, 13). "The Lord has established His throne in the heavens and His kingdom rules over all"

(103:13).[2]

The Throne of God

The Bible states: "Immediately I was in the Spirit; and behold, a throne was standing in heaven, and One sitting on the throne. And He who was sitting was like a jasper stone and a sardius in appearance; and there was a rainbow around the throne, like an emerald in appearance. Around the throne were twenty-four thrones; and upon the thrones I saw twenty-four elders sitting, clothed in white garments, and golden crowns on their heads. Out from the throne come flashes of lightning and sounds and peals of thunder. And there were seven lamps of fire burning before the throne, which are the seven Spirits of God; and before the throne there was something like a sea of glass, like crystal; and in the center and around the throne, four living creatures full of eyes in front and behind. The first creature was like a lion, and the second creature like a calf, and the third creature had a face like that of a man, and the fourth creature was like a flying eagle. And the four living creatures, each one of them having six wings, are full of eyes around and within; and day and night they do not cease to say, "HOLY, HOLY, HOLY IS THE LORD GOD, THE ALMIGHTY, WHO WAS AND WHO IS AND WHO IS TO COME." And when the living creatures give glory and honor

---

[2] Geoffrey W. Bromiley, *The International Standard Bbile Encyclopedia* (Grand Rapids: William B. Eerdmans Publishing House 1915), 24.

and thanks to Him who sits on the throne, to Him who lives forever and ever, the twenty-four elders will fall down before Him who sits on the throne, and will worship Him who lives forever and ever, and will cast their crowns before the throne, saying, "Worthy are You, our Lord and our God, to receive glory and honor and power; for You created all things, and because of Your will they existed, and were created" (Rev.4:2-11).

The scriptures go on to inform us: "I saw in the right hand of Him who sat on the throne a book written inside and on the back, sealed up with seven seals. And I saw a strong angel proclaiming with a loud voice, "Who is worthy to open the book and to break its seals?" And no one in heaven or on the earth or under the earth was able to open the book or to look into it. Then I began to weep greatly because no one was found worthy to open the book or to look into it; and one of the elders said to me, "Stop weeping; behold, the Lion that is from the tribe of Judah, the Root of David, has overcome so as to open the book and its seven seals." And I saw between the throne (with the four living creatures) and the elders a Lamb standing, as if slain, having seven horns and seven eyes, which are the seven Spirits of God, sent out into all the earth. And He came and took the book out of the right hand of Him who sat on the throne. When He had taken the book, the four living creatures and the twenty-four elders fell down before the Lamb, each one holding a harp and golden bowls full of incense, which are the prayers of the saints. And they sang a new song, saying, "Worthy are You to take the book and to break its seals; for You were slain, and purchased for God with Your blood men from every tribe and tongue and people and nation. "You have made them to be a kingdom and priests to our God; and they will reign upon the earth" (Rev. 5:1-10).

And lastly: "Then he showed me a river of the water of life, clear as crystal, coming from the throne of God and of the Lamb, in the middle of its street. On either side of the river was the tree of life, bearing twelve kinds of fruit, yielding its fruit every month; and the leaves of the tree were for the healing of the nations. There will no longer be any curse; and the throne of God and of the Lamb will be in it, and His bond-servants will serve Him; they will see His face, and His name will be on their foreheads. And there will no longer be any night; and they will not have need of the light of a lamp nor the light of the sun, because the Lord God will illumine them; and they will reign forever and ever. And he said to me, "These words are faithful and true"; and the Lord, the God of the spirits of the prophets, sent His angel to show to His bond-servants the things which must soon take place. "And behold, I am coming quickly. Blessed is he who heeds the words of the prophecy of this book" (Rev. 22:1-7).

The City

God's infallible Word can help us with our perspective. It states: "The angel who talked with me had a measuring rod of gold to measure the city, its gates and its walls. The city was laid out like a square, as long as it was wide. He measured the city with the rod and found it to be 12,000 stadia in length, and as wide and high as it is long. He measured its wall and it was 144 cubits thick, by man's measurement, which the angel was using. The wall was made of jasper, and the city of pure gold, as pure as glass. The foundations of the city walls were decorated with every kind of precious stone. The first foundation was jasper, the second sapphire, the third chalcedony, the fourth emerald, the fifth sardonyx, the sixth carnelian, the seventh chrysolite, the eighth beryl, the ninth topaz, the tenth chryso-prase, the eleventh jacinth, and the twelfth amethyst. The twelve gates were twelve pearls, each gate made of a single pearl. The great street of the city was of pure gold, like transparent glass. I did not see a temple in the city, because the Lord God Almighty and the Lamb are its temple. The city does not need the sun or the moon to shine on it, for the glory of God gives it light, and the Lamb is its lamp. The nations will walk by its light, and the kings of the earth will bring their splendor into it. On no day will its gates ever be shut, for there will be no night there. The glory and honor of the nations will be brought into it. Nothing impure will ever enter it, nor will anyone who does what is shameful or deceitful, but only those whose names are written in the Lamb's book of life" (Rev. 21:15-27).

The Kingdom of God is Power

We learn what the kingdom of God is not in the book of First Corinthians, chapter four in verse twenty: "Sometimes when we learn what the kingdom of God is not, it explains more perfectly what it is. 'For the kingdom of God is not in word, but in power.' What does this indicate? It would indicate that the kingdom of God is vibrant. The kingdom of God is action. This kingdom of God is life. The kingdom of God is creative. If the kingdom of God is in power, this means the kingdom of God could be presently alive, active and functioning. Where God is, His presence is emanating life, healing, deliverance or heaven's powers."[3]

The Kingdom of God:
The Already But not Yet

"The 'mystery of the kingdom' is the key to the understanding of the unique element in Jesus' teaching about the kingdom. He announced that the kingdom of God had come near; in fact, He affirmed that it had actually come upon men (Mt. 12:28). It's important to note that in His response to John's disciples, Jesus was claiming that the fulfillment of the Old Testament hope with its attendant blessings was in fact *present* in His person and ministry. The fulfillment, however, was not taking place along expected lines, hence John's

---

[3] Gerald Derstine, *The Kingdom of God is at Hand* (Bradenton: Gospel Crusade Publications 1973), 6.

perplexity. The unexpected element was that fulfillment was taking place in Jesus, but without the eschatological consummation. The Old Testament prophetic hope of the coming Messianic kingdom of God as promised to Israel is being fulfilled in the person and ministry of Jesus, but not consummated. The Jews of our Lord's Day, in keeping with what they saw in the Old Testament, expected the consummation of the kingdom, the complete and final overthrow of Israel's political enemies and the ushering in of the age of blessed peace and prosperity in the land. Our Lord, however, came with the message that before the kingdom would come in its eschatological consummation it has come in His own person and work in spirit and power. The kingdom, therefore, is both the present spiritual reign of God and the future realm over which He will rule in power and glory."[4]

The Kingdom of Heaven versus The Kingdom of God

"The term "kingdom of Heaven" denotes realm from whence the kingdom comes, or whence is the kingdom as a place, realm, location and condition.

The term "kingdom of God" denotes whose is the kingdom, as a person. Who did the kingdom come from? Whose is the kingdom? Naturally we say it is God. We say that God is a

---

[4] The Kingdom of God: The Already But not Yet
www.enjoyinggodministries.com

person and believe He is a divine being, so the term "kingdom of God" denotes basically the person.

You would not have a kingdom of Heaven without God. It is impossible to have the kingdom of Heaven without God's presence; so if there is a kingdom of Heaven, God is there also. On the other hand, if you believe God exists as a Spirit as the Bible says, then there must be a measure of heaven within this Godly presence.

God is love. Love is in Heaven. So if you have the kingdom of God you also have the kingdom of Heaven right there. God's presence is a heavenly realm radiating peace, love, joy, faith, temperance, meekness, gentleness, wisdom, knowledge, understanding – "the fruit of the Spirit" (See Gal. 5:24-25). He is all that is great, perfect and mighty.

God's kingdom will basically and primarily be made in God's likeness. God is Spirit (See Jn. 4:24). Therefore, His kingdom will be primarily spiritual. Remember, we believe spiritual realities are more real than physical, because the physical is temporal, mortal, while the spiritual is eternal, immortal."[5]

The Kingdom of Darkness

While we've explored the notion of what is and is not the kingdom of God, let's

---

[5] Gerald Derstine, *The Kingdom of God is at Hand* (Bradenton: Gospel Crusade Publications 1973), 3.

also examine the other existent kingdom — the kingdom of darkness, whose head is the devil. Satan is called "the god of this age" and "the prince of this world" (2 Cor. 4:4; Jn. 12:31; 16:11). "He rules an organization of demonic beings and fallen man, which establishes a counter-culture of sin opposed to God's righteous order. The enemy has so entrenched the world's value systems, that the Bible speaks of earthly, natural wisdom as demonic (Jas. 3:14-15). The rulers of this world, following the wisdom of this world, crucified the Lord of glory (1 Cor. 2:4-8). John also discusses the evil present in the world in I John 2:16-17. He speaks of certain aspects of our "human culture" as being "not from the Father, but from the world."[6] Let's go to some of Masters teachings on this subject matter.

Some of Jesus' Teachings Regarding The Kingdom of Darkness

1. "Jesus says that the punishment of hell is so severe that it would be better for a person to lose an eye or a hand rather than that these members of the body should be instruments of sins that would lead to hell. Twice He speaks about the whole body being thrown into hell (Mt. 5:29, 30).

2. Jesus states that God has the power to "destroy both soul and body in hell" (Mt. 10:28).

3. In the Parable of the Talents, Jesus

---

[6] The Kingdom of Darkness www.seekye1.com

again uses the phrases "outer darkness" and "weep and gnash their teeth" (Mt. 25:30). In the Parable of the Sheep and the Goats, Jesus says to those whom He condemns, "Depart from Me, you cursed, into the eternal fire prepared for the devil and his angels" (25:41). Later in the same parable, Jesus describes their fate as "eternal punishment" (v. 46).

4. In several passages, Jesus implies that there will be degrees of punishment in hell. He speaks of hypocrites as those who will "receive the greater condemnation" (Mk. 12:40), and Jesus speaks of some who will receive "a severe beating," whereas others who have a lesser knowledge of the master's will, receive "a light beating" (Lk. 12:47, 48).[7]

The Names of Satan

"The Bible calls Satan by many different names. Each name has a slightly different meaning. The many other names for Satan give a fuller picture of who Satan is and what he does. There are more names for Satan in the Bible than for anyone else except Jesus Christ.

These Names Include:

Abaddon (trans. "Destruction") - Revelation 9:11
Accuser - Revelation 12:10
Adversary - 1 Peter 5:8
Angel of light - Corinthians 11:14

---

[7] Merril C. Tenney, *The Zondervan Pictorial Encyclopedia of the Bible* (Grand Rapids: Zondervan 1975), 115.

Angel of the bottomless pit - Revelation 9:11
Anointed covering cherub - Ezekiel 28:14
Antichrist - 1 John 4:3
Apollyon (trans. "the Destroyer") - Revelation 9:11
Beast - Revelation 14:9,10
Beelzebub (i.e., prince of demons) - Matthew 12:24
Belial (i.e., worthless) - 2 Corinthians 6:15
Deceiver - Revelation 12:9
Devil - 1 John 3:8
Dragon - Revelation 12:9
Enemy - Matthew 13:39
Evil one - John 17:15
Father of lies - John 8:44
God of this age - 2 Corinthians 4:4
King of Babylon - Isaiah 14:4
King of the bottomless pit - Revelation 9:11
King of Tyre - Ezekiel 28:12
Lawless one - 2 Thessalonians 2:8-10
Leviathan - Isaiah 27:1
Liar - John 8:44
Little horn - Daniel 8:9-11
Lucifer - Isaiah 14:12-14
Man of sin - 2 Thessalonians 2:3,4
Murderer - John 8:44
Power of darkness - Colossians 1:13, 14
Prince of the power of the air - Ephesians 2:1,2
Roaring lion - 1 Peter 5:8
Rulers of the darkness - Ephesians 6:12
Ruler of demons - Luke 11:15
Ruler of this world - John 12:31,32
Satan - Mark 1:13
Serpent of old - Revelation 12:9
Son of perdition - 2 Thessalonians 2:3,4
Star - Revelation 9:1
Tempter - Matthew 4:3

Thief - John 10:10
Wicked one - Ephesians 6:16"[8]

All Untruth Is Satanic

As we can see, Satan is a fraud and the many titles he holds confirm it. He is described as the liar and the father of lies. "All untruth is an abomination to God. God has consigned all liars to the lake of fire; He has excluded from the New Jerusalem everything that makes a lie. God hates everything that is not true. God hates everything that is not true, and true right through and through like Himself. He must have truth in the *inward* parts.

Let us dwell for a moment upon this clause "the *inward* parts." You will detect in Psalm 51 that that is running right through. Here it is: "create in me a clean *heart*"; "renew a right *spirit* within me"; "a broken *spirit* and a contrite *heart* you will not despise."

You see, it is all this innermost realm of things that has now arisen as the *real* need. No more deception, no more falsehood, no more mockery, no more make-believe, no more going on as though it is all right when it is not all right; no more using external means to cover over inward unreality; no more going to meetings, and saying prayers, and joining in the whole system, when the *inward* parts are not right before God.

Seeing then that we are what we are by nature now, this represents a re-constituting of

---

[8] The mark of the beast www.markbeast.com

us, therefore, anything that does not minister to that is false in itself. Any system of religion that just puts on from the outside, and covers over the inner life by mere rite and ritual is false, it is not true."[9] God hates anything that is counterfeit. That's why it's critical to "seek first His kingdom and His righteousness, and all these things will be added to you" (Mt. 6:33).

---

[9] T. Austin Sparks, *Truth in the Inward Parts* (Tulsa: Emmanuel Church 2001), 7.

NO ONE
GREATER THAN JOHN

The infallible Word of God informs us: "After John's messengers left, Jesus began to speak to the crowd about John: 'What did you go out into the desert to see? A reed swayed by the wind? If not, what did you go out to see? A man dressed in fine clothes? No, those who wear expensive clothes and indulge in luxury are in palaces. But what did you go out to see? A prophet? Yes, I tell you, and more than a prophet. This is the one about whom it is written: "I will send my messenger ahead of you, who will prepare your way before you." I tell you, among those born of women there is no one greater than John; yet the one who is least in the kingdom of God is greater than he'" (Lk. 7:24-28).

Now this statement that no one is greater than John has arrested my attention. I need to search the scriptures to see what John was doing. The Word of God for faith and conduct informs me: "Now in those days John the Baptist came, preaching in the wilderness of Judea, saying, 'Repent, for the kingdom of heaven is at hand.' For this is the one referred to by Isaiah the prophet when he said, 'THE VOICE OF ONE CRYING IN THE WILDERNESS, MAKE READY THE WAY OF THE LORD, MAKE HIS PATHS STRAIGHT!' Now John himself had a garment of camel's hair and a leather belt around his waist; and his food was locusts and wild honey. Then Jerusalem was going out to him, and all Judea and all the district around the Jordan; and they were being baptized by him in the Jordan River, as they confessed their sins. But when he saw many of the Pharisees and Sadducees coming for baptism, he said to them, 'You brood of vipers, who warned you to flee from the wrath to come'" (Mt. 3:1-7)?

John was preaching: "repent for the kingdom of Heaven is at hand." Wow, that's what I preached to the two teenagers in the restaurant last night! Therefore, if Jesus informs us, "there is no one greater than John," maybe we should be doing what John did. If and when we do witness to individuals regarding the kingdom of Heaven, we must make sure our motives are right. The Bible says, "Let all that you do be done in love" (1 Cor. 16:14). Do you know why John called the Pharisees and Sadducees a brood of vipers? While their 'coming out to be baptized by him' was the proper thing to do, their motives were in question.

As we know from scripture, John the Baptist was in the wilderness preaching and prophesying. He prophesied that someone mightier than him was coming to baptize them with fire. Let's look at the book of Matthew to see exactly what John stated. It says, "As for me, I baptize you with water for repentance, but He who is coming after me is mightier than I, and I am not fit to remove His sandals; He will baptize you with the Holy Spirit and fire. His winnowing fork is in His hand, and He will thoroughly clear His threshing floor; and He will gather His wheat into the barn, but He will burn up the chaff with unquenchable fire" (Mt. 3:11).

So John the Baptist was baptizing in the wilderness. And we're informed, "In those days Jesus came from Nazareth in Galilee and was baptized by John in the Jordan. Immediately coming up out of the water, He saw the heavens opening, and the Spirit like a dove descending upon Him; and a voice came out of the heavens: 'You are My beloved Son, in You I am well-pleased.' Immediately the Spirit impelled Him to go out into the wilderness. And He was in the wilderness forty days being tempted by Satan; and He was with the wild beasts, and the angels were ministering to Him" (Mk. 1:9-13 NAS).

I like that word impelled. Allow me to define that for you. It means: "1) to urge or drive forward 2) to impart motion to 3) propel."[10] The New American Standard uses the word "impelled," which I like to use when the Lord has me preach on this subject matter.

During these forty days of testing in the desert, we learn of the many trials Jesus went through. It's important to note that every time Satan tempted Him He quoted scripture to him. He would say: "It is written." or "It is said." Jesus always quoted the book of Deuteronomy (the second telling of the law) to Satan. It's vital we also quote scriptures when tempted.

---

[10] Merriam-Webster Online www.merriam-webster.com

So what is the first thing that happens after forty days of testing in the desert without food? Jesus begins His ministry and the very first thing the Bible states that takes place is this: "Now after John had been taken into custody, Jesus came into Galilee, preaching the gospel of God, and saying, 'The time is fulfilled, and the kingdom of God is at hand; repent and believe in the gospel'" (Mk. 1:15).

Jesus has not come back for the church yet, has He? Is Jesus' ministry still going forward on earth? Has the message changed? Do we need to inform others to repent, believe in the gospel because the kingdom of God is at hand? Are you willing to let Jesus' ministry work through you to a sick and dying world?

If you were to incorporate into your daily life the same principles and practices as John the Baptist and witness to others, Jesus may say there is no one greater than you, as long as it's done in love.

The early church didn't have big buildings, all kinds of programs, and big money sound equipment; yet, they turned the world upside down for the glory of God. What was it the early disciples did that changed the world? What did Jesus instruct them to do that we must know about? Let's go to the Word of truth and find out. It states: "These twelve Jesus sent out after instructing them: 'Do not go in the way of the Gentiles, and do not enter any city of the Samaritans; but rather go to the lost sheep of the house of Israel. And as you go, preach, saying, The kingdom of heaven is at hand'" (Mt. 10:5-7).

NICODEMUS

Once again let's turn to the scriptures to another Bible character named Nicodemus. "Now there was a man of the Pharisees, named Nicodemus, a ruler of the Jews; this man came to Jesus by night and said to Him, 'Rabbi, we know that You have come from God as a teacher; for no one can do these signs that You do unless God is with him'" (Jn. 3:1-2). What was Nicodemus asking Jesus? Wasn't he asking Jesus how do you operate in the kingdom of God? Wasn't he asking Jesus how do you operate in God's power here on earth? Nicodemus was a Pharisee and a ruler of the Jews. He was inquiring about the signs Jesus was performing with God. Individuals were witnessing Jesus being moved by compassion feeding the multitudes, healing outcast lepers and raising the dead.

We must operate in the kingdom of God the same way Jesus did, in love, motivated by compassion. The Bible records: "And Jesus called His disciples to Him, and said, 'I feel compassion for the people, because they have remained with Me now three days and have nothing to eat; and I do not want to send them away hungry, for they might faint on the way'" (Mt. 15:32). The Master then took seven loaves and a few small fish and fed four thousand. Seven full baskets were left over after they all ate and were satisfied. In the book of Mark it states: "When Jesus went ashore, He saw a large crowd, and He felt compassion for them because they were like sheep without a shepherd; and He began to teach them many things" (Mk. 6:34).

My favorite scriptures regarding Jesus being moved by compassion are found in the book of Matthew. The Bible says: "As they were leaving Jericho, a large crowd followed Him. And two blind men sitting by the road, hearing that Jesus was passing by, cried out, 'Lord, have mercy on us, Son of David!' The crowd sternly told them to be quiet, but they cried out all the more, 'Lord, Son of David, have mercy on us!' And Jesus stopped and called them, and said, 'What do you want Me to do for you?' They said to Him, 'Lord, we want our eyes to be opened.' Moved with compassion, Jesus touched their eyes; and immediately they regained their sight and followed Him" (Mt. 20:29-34).

Did you notice when Nicodemus came to Jesus it states, "this man came to Jesus by night." Nicodemus was concerned that others might observe him going to Jesus. In order to serve in the kingdom of God with power motivated by love and compassion, we must not fear men but God alone.

Let's look at another Jew, a man who was placed in a position of authority like Nicodemus. "One of the synagogue officials named Jairus came up, and on seeing Him, fell at His feet and implored Him earnestly, saying, 'My little daughter is at the point of death; please come and lay Your hands on her, so that she will get well and live'" (Mk. 5:22-23). It states that he fell at the feet of Jesus and implored Him earnestly. Wow! That's humility. He didn't sneak around at night? It doesn't appear he was concerned about what people thought, does it?

Back at that time when a Jew converted to Christianity and started following Jesus most would leave their businesses if they had one. The Jews would no longer do business with them once they converted to Christianity. Their family would disown them and they would be mocked by the Jewish community. Many social, physical, mental and emotional changes would be involved. Isn't that still the case at this present time in many cases when an individual joins the family of God?

God has used thousands of individuals to assist me. Many have been put in my life for a day, a week, for a season or two, some until a certain goal or situation was met or accomplished. It seems ministers have hurt me the most when they informed me they would help me down the road. They may have meant well at the time. Ministers must be very careful not to make promises they can't keep because people look up to them. Then, when the time comes, their help was not available. I allowed myself to be hurt because I was trusting in them and not in God fully. We also have to be careful because pride can also play a big role in being offended. I haven't found in scripture were it says that Satan and his host take naps.

I have recently heard a sermon by Bishop TD Jakes that has helped me so much regarding the individuals that God puts in my life. He stated they are our confidants, constituents or our comrades.

1)   "**Confidants** – There will be very few of them. They are into you whether you're up or down, right or wrong. They are into you. They will come to see you in the prison or get you out of the crack house. You'll never inherit your kingdom until you find your confidant. You can't be David until you find your Jonathan.

2)   **Constituents** – They are for what you are for. As long as you are for what they are for they will walk with you and work with you and labor with you. However, never think they are for you. They are for what you are for. Because if they meet someone else that will further their agenda they will leave you and hook up with them because they were never for you. They were for what you were for. They are your constituents. Throughout your life if you're not careful, particularly if you're broken you will mistake your constituents for your confidants. And by the time you get done falling in love with them they will break your heart because it was never about you anyway, it's about the causes you represent. They are what you are for but they are not for you, they are you constituents.

3)   **Comrades** – These people are not for you nor are they for what you are for. They are against what you are against. Comrades will make strange bedfellows. This will cause people to come together who are not for you, but they are against what you are against. They

will team up with you to fight the enemy. Don't be confused by their association. They will only be with you until the victory is accomplished. These people are like scaffolding. They come into your life to fulfill a purpose and when the purpose is complete the scaffolding is removed. But don't be upset when they are removed because the purpose has been fulfilled. The building stays standing when the scaffolding is removed. Expect constituents and comrades to leave you after awhile. Don't get upset when they don't react to your dream the way you expected them to because they were never really with you in the first place. Be careful then who you tell your dream to. If you tell your dream to constituents they will desert you and fulfill the dream without you. If you tell it to your comrades they won't support it because they were never for what you were for anyway. If you find a few people in your entire life with who you can share your dream with, you are a blessed. I can tell you how you can identify people who are really for you. If they are really for you, they will weep with you, when you weep. And they will rejoice with you when you rejoice. When you walk into a room and tell people good news, stop and watch their reaction. If they're not happy for you, shut your mouth and walk out of the room. Because when they are really connected to you, they will be happy for you when you share your dream."[11]

---

[11] Sermon by Bishop TD Jakes, *Five People in your Life* (accessed 30 May 2010) available from: http://www.youtube.com/watch?v=rZpcRemufO4&feature=related

As you can see from the aforementioned sermon, we must seek the Holy Spirit to find a balance regarding the extent to which we put our trust in a certain individual. We are to put our full trust in God and fear Him. I hope and pray you have drawn vital conclusions from this chapter and that you are aware of the following statement: "In order to operate in the kingdom of God, with the power of God, we must be motivated by love and compassion, and lastly fear and trust God."

ACTS 10:38

I am an evangelist at heart. Any and all evangelists have to absolutely love the following verse: "You know of Jesus of Nazareth, how God anointed Him with the Holy Spirit and with power, and how He went about doing good and healing all who were oppressed by the devil, for God was with Him" (Acts 10:38). Another fundamental scripture is: "Jesus was going through all the cities and villages, teaching in their synagogues and proclaiming the gospel of the kingdom, and healing every kind of disease and every kind of sickness" (Mt. 9:35).

It is important to truly understand these verses so we can bear much fruit for God's kingdom. "Jesus Christ went about promoting the well-being of men wherever He went. He did what He could wisely do for the bodies of men, healing the sick, supplying physical wants; but more especially He sought to promote the highest spiritual good of the people, teaching, warning, rebuking and entreating, as circumstances seemed to require, evermore intent upon promoting the highest human happiness by every means in His power. His history shows amply how He did this.

Chapter 4

What is Implied in His Going About Doing Good?

It is implied that this was His business—the thing He had above all things else at heart. For this end He came into the world. He came to do good and not evil; to bless and not to curse; to fill the world with peace, love and happiness, so far as lay within the range of His influence. The good of man was the great object which He sought.

It is implied that Christ sought the happiness of mankind disinterestedly, in the sense that He valued their well-being, that He really loved it and enjoyed the efforts He made to promote it. He was truly and honestly benevolent. It was because He loved the happiness of men that He labored to promote it."[12]

To Destroy the Works of the Devil

Can I inform you why the Almighty God who sits on His throne sent His only beloved Son down here to this mess? It is written: "For this purpose the Son of God was manifested, that He might destroy the works of the devil" (1 Jn. 3:8 KJV). God sent Jesus here to destroy the works of the devil. Why did God send Jesus to live in you? He's in you for a purpose, to destroy the works of the devil. What will He do in you? The same works Jesus

---

[12] Jesus Christ Doing Good by Charles G. Finney www.gospeltruth.net

did and greater works.

Wherever I go things change. When I walk into the post office it changes. When I walk into the supermarket it changes. Why? Because I am a child of God, walking in the Spirit of God and there is a powerful anointing on my life. Why? To defeat the work of the devil. Many times when I walk into an establishment the individuals in the place know it changed. Many times people as far as twenty feet away will turn around who had their back to me and look right at me. Why, because they felt the tangible presence of Almighty God. Especially individuals that are demon possessed.

If you are a child of God and are walking in the Spirit, and not the flesh, what was impossible before you walked into the room becomes possible. Why? Because the Lord can use you to transfer the anointing to individuals who had cancer and were on their way to the grave and be instantly healed. Wow! Destroying the works of the devil…

That scripture said Jesus "went about doing good and healing." You're always going. You're going to work. You're going to the post office. You're going to the supermarket. As you go, let the Lord use you to touch lives everywhere. Why is all this possible? Because the kingdom of God is at hand.

POPPING UP LIKE POPCORN

I want to share many testimonies and experiences with you; because if you get a hold of this, you will begin to see miracles popping up like popcorn on a regular basis. Individuals all over the universe are in need of a touch from heaven and the Lord wants to use the saints as His instruments to touch them.

However, before I do, I have a question for you. Why is operating in the gifts of the Spirit slow in some and quick in others? Let's talk about this first, because I want to challenge you some more.

Growing Up Into Him

It has to do with spiritual development. "The Christian life is not by effort, and not by struggle; not merely by trying to put into practice certain maxims, or by trying to attain to a certain measure; but from beginning to end, and all together, it is a matter of knowing the Lord Jesus *within*. Of course this implies response to Him, and a continual yieldedness to His working by His Spirit within, and so co-operating with Him in His purpose of conformity to His image.

Why is spiritual growth so slow in some and so gloriously quick in others? Because some kick and question, or argue with God; go round and round the point asking, does it mean this? Must I do this? Is it necessary? Can I, may

I do this, and so on. Yet these very people are loudest in saying they want only the will of God; but their very affirmation often shows a struggle is going on, and their growth is fraught with a good deal of friction.

Others in a beautiful sincerity and purity of Spirit are immediately letting go to the Lord, so He is able to lead them on, without waste of time in controversy with the will of God; and there is no weakness through there not being an utter abandonment and whole-hearted obedience and surrender to that will. There is a passion for the Lord Himself, and for Him to have His full way at whatever cost."[13] The more we yield to the Lord, the more He can use us and many more miracles will take place.

Pop, Pop, Pop

On a summer's day in New England back in 2005, I saw a gentleman walking toward me down the sidewalk with a terrible limp. I approached him and asked him if he would like the Lord to give him an instant miracle and heal his walking problem. He informed me he had a bad hip and he was interested in receiving a miracle. I put my hand on his hip and said: "In the name of Jesus, hip I command you to be healed. Pain and inflammation go now in Jesus' name. I then informed the man to run to a dumpster which was approximately forty feet down the sidewalk. He took off running. When

---

[13] T. Austin Sparks *The Measure of Christ* (Tulsa: Emmanuel Church 1998), 13.

he returned from his little jog, he informed me the Lord totally healed him. I then asked him would he like to receive Jesus as his Lord and Savior, the same Jesus that had just instantly healed his hip. We prayed together and he received Jesus Christ as his Lord and Savior. All glory to God!

Wow!

I was preaching on revival in Texas one evening. Toward the end of my sermon, I received a word of knowledge from the Holy Spirit. I approached a man in his late thirties who was seated at the back of the congregation and I asked him, "Do you have pain in your body?" He came out to the aisle and stated, "Since I was a teenager, I have had severe pain in my shoulders and ankles." He went on to say how he has been to every kind of doctor one could visit. I ask him if he was ready for a miracle and he said he was. I laid hands on his shoulders and said, "In the name of Jesus, shoulders I command you to be healed. Pain and inflammation go now in Jesus' name." I then prayed the exact same prayer for his ankles. I informed him the Lord healed him and then he started dancing and shouting pain free.

Two Spanish Pastors

In my last year of studies at Zion Bible College in Haverhill, MA, I discovered a Spanish church that held a Thursday evening service. The name of the church is Pentecostal

International Ministry and the pastor is Marilyn
Mendez. She is a very powerful woman of God.
She's from Puerto Rico and I have many good
memories from that church. Some weekends
the men would stay in the church all weekend
and fast and pray. I love that about the Spanish
churches.

I believe it was my second visit there
and the pastor's voice sounded awful. I asked
the Spanish woman who was sitting near me if
it was the intercom system or if it was the
pastor's voice. She stated it was her voice. After
the service, when she was finished talking with
everyone, I asked her if I could pray for her. She
said that would be nice. I put my hand on her
throat and said, "In the name of my Jesus,
throat I command you to be healed. Pain and
inflammation go now in Jesus' name." She
received an instant miracle. She was delighted
the Lord healed her.

The following morning the Holy Spirit
told me to go back to that church and give
Pastor Marilyn two hundred and fifty dollars. I
only had two hundred and seventy dollars to
my name and I got very excited. I was certain
the devil would never tell me to give money to
a pastor so I knew God was up to something
big. I couldn't wait to get back to that church
and sow that seed as the Lord instructed.

At the following service, a guest speaker
was visiting. Her voice was also very raspy.
After the service, I put my hand on her throat
and said, "In the name of my Jesus, throat I
command you to be healed. Pain and
inflammation go now in Jesus' name." She also

received an instant miracle. She was delighted the Lord instantly touched her.

After the service, I took out my checkbook and found out how to spell the pastor's name. I gave her that financial blessing. The following morning while walking to my second class at 8:50 am my phone rang. The individual on the other end informed me they had a check for me for $15,000 for my tuition for that year. Oh, praise God everybody who is reading this! Hallelujah!

Holy Ghost Fire

I was asked by a pastor who was going out of town if I could preach a ten o'clock Sunday morning service in his place. I did and I preached on Hebrews chapter four. The verses are: "Therefore, let us fear if, while a promise remains of entering His rest, any one of you may seem to have come short of it. For indeed we have had good news preached to us, just as they also; but the word they heard did not profit them, because it was not united by faith in those who heard" (Heb. 4:1-2).

I preached on all the verses in that chapter that talk about entering God's rest. As you know, God will always confirm His Word. After the service, everyone left the building and an older woman approached me. She stated she had severe pain in both her arms and all the hospitals in McAllen, Texas couldn't tell her what the problem was. She asked me if I would pray for her.

I asked her to raise her arms up. I then

grabbed her arms at the wrists. I took a deep breath and just rested. When I rested, she sensed it. Then she rested and her heart connected with the anointing. Then she started screaming, "I'm on fire! I'm on fire! My arms are burning up!" I told her, "The Lord is a consuming fire; He's healing you." She then started yelling, "He's healing my neck too! I'm on fire!" Praise God!

I want you to understand something very important. This is not something that only the pastor or evangelist does. This is for the entire body of Christ. The first man I told you about with the hip problem, well I was saved about a year and one week baptized in the Holy Spirit when that miracle took place. The Lord will most always heal an unbeliever. He wants to show Himself strong in an unbeliever's life. I heard evangelist Ted Shuttlesworth say, "Miracles are the dinner bells the Lord uses to call people to His banquet table."

Obedience to the Holy Spirit

The Word of God informs us that Jesus used mud pies and a man received his sight. We must be open and obedient to the Holy Spirit because we never know how someone may receive their healing. I went down to Victoria, Mexico with my friend Charley Elliott from Soul Harvest Missions. It's about a five hour drive in from the U. S. border. The church seats about four thousand and it was half full on a Sunday morning. At the end of the sermon, Pastor Bobby Crow informed the congregation that if anyone needed a miracle they were to come forward and Charley and I would pray for them.

Many individuals received healing. However, one young man about twenty-four years of age told me he was deaf in his left ear. I put my fingers in his ears and commanded evil sprits to come out in Jesus' name and nothing happened. Then I heard the Holy Spirit tell me to slap him. When you have two thousand people in the audience watching you, it's a different ballgame than ministering on the sidewalk. I never ministered in a church that size. However, as soon as I slapped him in his left ear, he received perfect hearing. Why did he receive this instant miracle? He received it because the kingdom of God is at hand.

Let's not forget the fact that God is sovereign. It's one of His many divine attributes. He can do what He wants, when He wants, and how He wants to do it. We must be sensitive to the Holy Spirit. Let's not forget, many individuals on this earth need a touch from heaven. Wow, are those dinner bells I'm hearing?

In so many cases, when individuals receive a healing touch from the Master, they have been inflicted for weeks, months and possibly many years. Giving a testimony after receiving a healing or healings is very important. Many evangelists who the Lord uses will ask the individuals who receive healing to meet them at the next location, to give their testimony. Giving your testimony may be at times part of the process to maintain your healing. Revelations 12:11 informs us: "We overcome by the blood of the Lamb and by the Word of our testimony." With that in mind, please enjoy the following devotion by Charles Spurgeon:

He that was Healed
Wist not Who it Was. - John 5:13

"Years are short to the happy and healthy; but thirty-eight years of disease must have dragged a very weary length along the life of the poor impotent man. When Jesus, therefore, healed him by a word, while he lay at the pool of Bethesda, he was delightfully sensible of a change. Even so the sinner who has for weeks and months been paralyzed with despair, and has wearily sighed for salvation, is very conscious of the change when the Lord Jesus speaks the word of power, and gives joy and peace in believing. The evil removed is too great to be removed without our discerning it; the life imparted is too remarkable to be possessed and remain inoperative; and the change wrought is too marvelous not to be perceived. Yet the poor man was ignorant of the author of his cure; he knew not the sacredness of His person, the offices which He sustained, or the errand which brought Him among men. Much ignorance of Jesus may remain in hearts which yet feel the power of His blood. We must not hastily condemn men for lack of knowledge; but where we can see the faith which saves the soul, we must believe that salvation has been bestowed. The Holy Spirit makes men penitents long before He makes them divines; and he who believes what he knows, shall soon know more clearly what he believes. Ignorance is, however, an evil; for this poor man was much tantalized by the Pharisees, and was quite unable to cope with them. It is good to be able to answer gainsayers; but we cannot do so if we know not the Lord Jesus clearly and with understanding. The cure of his ignorance, however, soon followed the cure of his infirmity, for he was visited by the Lord in the temple; and after that gracious manifestation, he was found testifying that "it was Jesus who had made him whole." Lord, if Thou hast saved me, show me Thyself, that I may declare Thee to the sons of men."[14]

---

[14] Spurgeon's Morning by Morning
www.ewordtoday.com

Chapter 6

THE MINISTRY OF RECONCILIATION

Let us go to God's Word to see how blessed we are. It is written: "Therefore if anyone is in Christ, he is a new creature; the old things passed away; behold, new things have come. Now all these things are from God, who reconciled us to Himself through Christ and gave us the ministry of reconciliation, namely, that God was in Christ reconciling the world to Himself, not counting their trespasses against them, and He has committed to us the word of reconciliation. Therefore, we are ambassadors for Christ, as though God were making an appeal through us" (2 Cor. 5:17-20).

I'm a new creature in Christ Jesus. That makes me want to shout! It goes on to say Jesus has given us the ministry to inform others about Him. Before I get too excited, let's pray. Father, I thank you for your Word. I thank you for the breath of life and this day you have made. Father, in Jesus' name, I ask that you will open our understanding and fill us with godly wisdom regarding being an ambassador of reconciliation for the kingdom of God. Amen.

If I were to hang around the church parking lot after a service and ask individuals what ministry the Lord has given them, many would probably say things like, "I serve in the bookstore," "I'm an usher," or "I play the drums." All these things are wonderful;

however, my point is how many people would say, "Jesus has given me the ministry of reconciliation and I am to inform others about the love of Christ"?

Many times in my own life when I think of sin, I do not think about the sin of silence. So many times when I'm out in society I could do a lot better ministering as I go from place to place. The Bible says: "For by your words you will be justified, and by your words you will be condemned" (Mt. 12:37). Not only will we be judged by what we said wrong, we will also be judged by what we didn't say at all. Let's look at a parable and see what Jesus says regarding the kingdom of God.

"And He was saying, 'The kingdom of God is like a man who casts seed upon the soil; and he goes to bed at night and gets up by day, and the seed sprouts and grows — how, he himself does not know. The soil produces crops by itself; first the blade, then the head, then the mature grain in the head. But when the crop permits, he immediately puts in the sickle, because the harvest has come'" (Mk. 4:26-29).

I know you want to read about the kingdom of God because that's what's on the front cover. Now, the key is to apply the knowledge we obtain from this material. Wisdom is applied knowledge. I find the following information of much interest.

So is the Kingdom of God

"The inward kingdom is like seed which a man casts into the ground - This a preacher of the Gospel casts into the heart. And he sleeps and rises night and day - That is, he has it continually in his thoughts. Meantime it springs and grows up he knows not how - Even he that sowed it cannot explain how it grows. For as the earth by a curious kind of mechanism, which the greatest philosophers cannot comprehend, does as it were spontaneously bring forth first the blade, then the ear, then the full corn in the ear: so the soul, in an inexplicable manner, brings forth, first weak graces, then stronger, then full holiness: and all this of itself, as a machine, whose spring of motion is within itself. Yet observe the amazing exactness of the comparison. The earth brings forth no corn (as the soul no holiness) without both the care and toil of man, and the benign influence of heaven."[15]

I hope you see the importance of us to become farmers for the Lord Jesus and cast seed into the hearts of others. Sometimes it may start with making a decision like, "No matter what, I will tell at least one individual about Jesus every day." That's a start. Or maybe it would be to dedicate three hours every Saturday morning and witness at the mall, the park, or the beach. Years ago, when I first started witnessing to others, what helped me was a printable tract which is available at: www.revival.com.

I have witnessed to thousands of individuals and I feel I have to share this with you. I was in my second year of Bible College.

---

[15] Wesley's Explanatory Notes
www.biblestudytools.com

Chapter 6

At that time, I lived six miles from the college and was computing daily. One particular morning during my drive, I happened to be in sin and was feeling really bad. When I got to a red light, I heard someone blowing the horn. I looked over and saw a women smiling and waving who had prayed with me to receive Jesus as her Lord.

This made me feel so convicted and I informed the Lord He had a real sense of humor. I got to the second light and heard another horn. I looked and it was a gentlemen waving and smiling who prayed to receive Jesus with me also. I got to the third light and a different woman who received Jesus with me blew her horn. That's the type of thing that can happen when you witness to others as you go about your day.

When I got in the chapel at school, I went right to the altar. I was feeling like I had let my Lord down; I was a man who preached one thing and lived another... And do you know what the Lord said to me? He said, "I am so proud of the progress you have made (even though I turned my back on Him and was in sin)." I couldn't stop crying because of the unconditional love of God I was receiving. I got the attention of my dear friend Rev. John Blondo, a very sensitive and caring man of God, who was on the platform. John has been mentoring me for years. I shared it with him and I could not stop crying.

The point I have to make is this. When you have a calling to be an ambassador of reconciliation on your life and you minister life

51

to others as you go through your day, God will use you to change communities for His glory. Do you want to know why? Because the kingdom of God is at Hand!

THE SUFFERING SERVANT

Before I embark on this chapter, I feel there is something I should highlight. "The words of Jesus about the blood of the covenant implicitly claim that this promise of the new covenant in the kingdom of God is about to be fulfilled through His own death. Jesus looked forward beyond death to the perfect fellowship of the consummated kingdom. The meal symbolized the messianic banquet in the kingdom of God, but it also symbolized Jesus' death. Thus His death and the coming of the kingdom are somehow inseparable."[16]

With that being said, I believe it may help us to have a greater appreciation for His suffering, His death, the kingdom of God, and this chapter.

HIS DESTINY

Exalted and Extolled

"Behold, my servant will prosper, He will be high and lifted up and greatly exalted" (Is. 52:13).

---

[16] Geoffrey w. Bromiley, *The International Standard Bible Encyclopedia* (Grand Rapids: William B. Eerdmans Publishing Company 1915), 28.

Great Humiliation

"Just as many were astonished at you, my people, so His appearance was marred more than any man and His form more than the sons of men" (Is. 52:14).

He Will Astonish Kings

"Thus He will sprinkle many nations, Kings will shut their mouths on account of Him; for what had not been told them they will see, and what they had not heard they will understand" (Is. 52:15).

HIS LIFE

Some Would Not Believe

"Who has believed our message? And to whom has the arm of the Lord been revealed" (Is. 53:1)?

Despised and Rejected

"He was despised and forsaken of men, A man of sorrows and acquainted with grief; and like one from whom men hide their face He was despised, and we did not esteem Him" (Is. 53:3).

54

Chapter 7

HIS SUFFERING

Bearing Our Sorrow, Smitten and Afflicted By God

"Surely our grief's He Himself bore, and our sorrows He carried; yet we ourselves esteemed Him stricken, smitten of God, and afflicted" (Is. 53:4).

His Wounds Allowed our Forgiveness and Healing

"But He was pierced through for our transgressions, He was crushed for our iniquities; the chastening for our well-being fell upon Him, and by His scourging we are healed" (Is. 53:5).

Our Sins Were Put On Him

"All of us like sheep have gone astray, each of us has turned to his own way; but the Lord has caused the iniquity of us all to fall on Him" (Is. 53:6).

HIS SUBMISSION

He Did Not Say a Word

"He was oppressed and He was afflicted, yet He did not open His mouth; like a lamb that is led to slaughter, and like a sheep that is silent before its shearers, so He did not open His mouth" (Is. 53:7).

Chapter 7

Injured For Our Transgressions

"By oppression and judgment He was taken away; and as for His generation, who considered that He was cut off out of the land of the living for the transgression of my people, to whom the stroke was due" (Is. 53:8)?

HIS REWARD

The Lord Was Pleased

"But the Lord was pleased to crush Him, putting Him to grief; If He would render Himself as a guilt offering, He will see His offspring, He will prolong His days, and the good pleasure of the Lord will prosper in His hand" (Is. 53:10).

The Lord Was Satisfied

"As a result of the anguish of His soul, He will see it and be satisfied; by His knowledge the Righteous One, My Servant, will justify the many, as He will bear their iniquities" (Is. 53:11).

In conclusion: "The necessity for Jesus' death is further affirmed in His present role as the Suffering Servant. He who is destined to be the eschatological Son of man in the consummation of the kingdom is first of all the suffering Son of man who must suffer many things and be rejected by this generation" (Lk. 17:25). The essential relationship between Jesus' death and the coming of the kingdom is illustrated in that the sayings about His death refer to Him as the Son of man (Mk. 8:31; 9:31; 10:33f.). The Son of man by definition was an apocalyptic figure in the eschatological consummation (Dd. 7:13f.). Before He fulfills His eschatological role, however, the Son of man must appear on earth in a mission of humility and suffering as the Servant of the Lord, to give His life as a ransom for many (Mk 10:45). The eschatological consummation is linked with what God is doing in history in Jesus, especially in His death."[17]

---

[17] Ibid, 28.

RIGHTOUSNESS AND JOY AND PEACE IN THE HOLY SPIRIT

Sermon by Pastor John Piper
Bethlehem Baptist Church

Romans 14:16-19

"'So do not let what you regard as good be spoken of as evil. For the kingdom of God is not a matter of eating and drinking but of righteousness and peace and joy in the Holy Spirit. Whoever thus serves Christ is acceptable to God and approved by men. So then let us pursue what makes for peace and for mutual upbuilding' (Ro. 14:16-19).

Romans 14 is a call mainly for the strong to love the weak. It goes the other way also. For example, in verse 3 Paul says, "Let not the one who eats despise the one who abstains, and let not the one who abstains pass judgment on the one who eats, for God has welcomed him." So both those who are free in their conscience to eat and those who aren't should learn how to love each other and how not to judge or despise each other. But mainly the chapter is addressed to the strong who are in danger of flaunting their freedom and causing the weak to stumble.

Chapter 8

Exhortations to the Strong

So the exhortations to the strong run through the chapter: Verse 13: "Decide never to put a stumbling block or hindrance in the way of a brother." Verse 15b: "Do not destroy the one for whom Christ died." Verse 20: "Do not, for the sake of food, destroy the work of God." Verse 21: "It is good not to eat meat or drink wine or do anything that causes your brother to stumble." Verse 22: "The faith that you have, keep between yourself and God." I left out a very important one in verse 19 because I want to end on it—it's a positive summary exhortation: "Let us pursue what makes for peace and for mutual upbuilding." We will come back to this.

Reasons Why These Exhortations Should Be Obeyed

Besides these exhortations mainly to the strong, the chapter is woven together with reasons that Paul gives for why these exhortations to love and not to destroy should be obeyed. For example, verse 9: Christ died to be Lord both of the dead and the living—how much more the strong and the weak! Verse 3b: Don't judge the brother because "God has welcomed him." Verse 10: Don't judge because "we will all stand before the judgment seat of God." Verse 6b: Don't judge or despise because it is possible to glorify God by eating and by abstaining: "The one who eats, eats in honor of the Lord, since he gives thanks to God, while the one who abstains, abstains in honor of the Lord and gives thanks to God."

Now Paul gives another reason why the strong should not flaunt their freedom and put stumbling blocks in the way of the weak. We see the exhortation in verse 16 and then the positive expression of it in verse 19. Verse 16: "So do not let what you regard as good be spoken of as evil." Verse 19: "So then let us pursue what makes for peace and for mutual upbuilding." Then between these two exhortations (the negative one in verse 16, the positive one in verse 19) he gives a reason that he has not mentioned before in this chapter. But it is deeply rooted in chapters 1–8.

He says in verse 17, "For the kingdom of God is not a matter of eating and drinking but of righteousness and peace and joy in the Holy Spirit." Then in verse 18 he confirms that serving Christ like that is indeed a manifestation of God's kingdom because it pleases God and wins serious approval from man. "Whoever thus serves Christ is acceptable to God and approved by men."

Don't Use Your Good
to Hurt Your Brother (v. 16)

So let's start with verse 16: "So do not let what you regard as good be spoken of as evil." Paul has just said in verse 15, "If your brother is grieved by what you eat, you are no longer walking in love. By what you eat, do not destroy the one for whom Christ died." Now he says, Therefore, "do not let what you regard as good be spoken of as evil." In other words, if you take your good faith and your good freedom and your good, clean food, and use it in away that causes a brother to be grieved, and possibly even destroyed, then your "good" faith and your "good" freedom and your "good, clean" food will not be praised. They will be spoken of as evil. In fact they will have become evil—you are no longer "walking in love" (v. 15). And lovelessness should be spoken of as evil.

So Paul says in verse 16: Don't do that. Don't let that happen. Don't use your good faith and your good liberty and your good, clean food that way. Why would you do that? And he gives the new reason now in verse 17 for why that makes no sense. Why would you think that your eating and drinking in liberty is so important that you must hurt your brother? Don't you know (v. 17) that "the kingdom of God is not a matter of eating and drinking but of righteousness and peace and joy in the Holy Spirit."

What Paul Means by "Kingdom of God"

This is the only place in the book of Romans where Paul uses the word "kingdom." But he uses it elsewhere and we can know what he means by "kingdom of God." Four clarifications:

1) **First, he means the reign of God, not the realm of God**. We tend to think of a kingdom as a place. But for Jesus and for Paul it almost

61

never has that meaning. Rather it means the reign or the rule of God. You can see that here: Where the Holy Spirit is bringing about righteousness and peace and joy, the kingdom (that is, the reign of God) is being manifested.

2) **The kingdom of God refers to his saving reign, not to His total providence over all things**. In one sense God reigns over all. So you could call everything "God's kingdom." But that is clearly not the way Paul uses the term. The kingdom of God is God's redemptive reign. His saving reign. When Jesus said to pray, "Hallowed by your name, your kingdom come, your will be done on earth as it is in heaven" (Matthew 6: 9-10), he meant that the coming of the kingdom would be the extent of God's rule where His name is hallowed and His will is done the way angels do it—obediently and joyfully. So the kingdom of God is God's reign, not realm; and it is His saving, redeeming reign bringing about the hallowing of His name and the joyful doing of his will.

3) **The kingdom of God is fulfilled partially in the present and will be consummated at the end of the age when Christ comes a second time**. Paul speaks of unbelievers not inheriting the kingdom of God (1 Corinthians 6:9), and so treats the kingdom as yet future. But then he also says to believers that "He has delivered us from the domain of darkness and transferred us to the kingdom of His beloved Son," and so treats the kingdom as already present.

4) **The kingdom of God and the kingdom of Christ are the same**. He says in Ephesians 5:5, "Everyone who is sexually immoral or impure, or who is covetous . . . has no inheritance in the kingdom of Christ and God." There is one kingdom, and it is the kingdom of Christ and of God. So to serve the kingdom of God is to serve Christ, and to serve Christ is to serve the kingdom of God.

So Paul is saying in verse 16, don't use your good—your good faith and your good liberty and your good food—to hurt anyone. Don't put that much weight on eating and drinking. It's not that crucial. Why? He answers in verse 17: Because "the kingdom of God is not a matter of eating and drinking but of righteousness and peace and joy in the Holy Spirit." The saving, redeeming, sanctifying rule of God—the kingdom of God—has broken into this world in Jesus Christ, the Messiah—the King—and the evidence of his rule in your lives is not eating and drinking. You may think that your liberty to eat all things is what God's kingdom produces. But that's not quite right. What the kingdom produces is something deeper and larger that governs how you use your liberty to eat all things.

Righteousness and Peace and Joy in the Holy Spirit

What does he mean that "the kingdom of God is . . . righteousness and peace and joy in the Holy Spirit"? That is not immediately obvious because Paul uses at least two of these terms in more than one way. Righteousness can mean the righteousness that God imputes to us when He declares us righteous through faith even when we are guilty sinners (Romans 4:5). And it can mean the righteousness that He then, on the basis of that right standing, begins to work in us (Romans 6:13, 16, 18, 19, 20). And peace can mean the peace that we have with God (Romans 5:1) or the peace we have with each other (2 Corinthians 13:11).

I am inclined to think Paul has in mind the second kind of righteousness and peace — namely, the kind that He works in us in relationship to each other. But it may be that he wants us to think of both and remember that our practical righteousness and peace that we work out with each other is built on the perfect righteousness that He imputes to us by faith alone and the peace that we enjoy with him.

I say this because it is remarkable how similar this sequence of righteousness, peace, and joy is with the sequence of thought in Romans 5:1-2. "Since we have been justified by faith [that is, declared righteous!], we have peace with God through our Lord Jesus Christ. Verse 2: "Through Him we have also obtained access by faith into this grace in which we stand, and we rejoice in hope of the glory of God." So there is righteousness imputed through faith, peace with God, and joy in the hope of His glory. So I wonder if Paul doesn't want us to have that in our mind as the basis of the righteousness and peace and joy that he refers to here in Romans 14:17.

What makes me think that he probably

is referring to our practical lived-out righteousness (rather than the imputed righteousness of Christ) and the practical-lived out peace with each other is the phrase "in the Holy Spirit." "The kingdom of God is... righteousness and peace and joy in the Holy Spirit." This seems to mean that the Holy Spirit is working these things right now. He is ruling in us to make us more righteous, more peaceable, and more joyful. This seems to be the fruit of the Spirit now, not a declarative act back at the beginning of our Christian lives. This work is built on justification by faith. But now the Spirit is producing in us these things: righteousness, peace, and joy.

That, Paul says, is the kingdom of God. In other words, the work of the Holy Spirit and the advancing of the kingdom of God are the same thing. This is exactly what we saw in the ministry of Jesus, for example, in Matthew 12:28. Jesus said, "If it is by the Spirit of God that I cast out demons, then the kingdom of God has come upon you." The work of the Spirit is the presence of the kingdom of God. Or to say it another way: The reign of God is exercised through His Spirit.

So when the Spirit rules and conquers our selfishness and pride, and replaces it with Christlike righteousness, then we will not grieve and destroy a brother for the sake of food. The Spirit of God — the kingdom of God — creates righteousness and peace and joy. This is what the Spirit of God does. He creates righteousness and peace and joy. And when you have these, you don't grieve and destroy a weaker brother.

Serving Christ in This Way Is Pleasing To God

Then, in verse 18, Paul confirms this by explaining that what he has just said is in fact what pleases God and wins the sober approval of others. "Whoever thus serves Christ is acceptable to God and approved by men." That is, whoever serves Christ in the way that verse 17 just described is pleasing to God.

What did verse 17 say? It said that righteousness comes "in the Holy Spirit." And when it comes "in — or by — the Holy Spirit," it is the kingdom of God coming. So if you serve Christ that way, you please God. What does that mean? What is it here that pleases God? What pleases God is not just when we serve Christ — not just when we try to do the righteousness that he commands — but when we do it in a certain way. And that way is described in verse 17 as "in the Holy Spirit."

There is a way to serve Christ that would dishonor Christ. That's why Jesus said in Mark 10:45, "The Son of Man came not to be served but to serve, and to give His life as a ransom for many." There is a way to serve Christ that would dishonor Him. And there is a way to serve God that would dishonor God. That's why Paul said in Acts 17:25, "Neither is God served by human hands, as though He needed anything, since He himself gives to all mankind life and breath and everything."

The way to serve Christ and God so that

they are dishonored is to serve with the mindset that they need you. They are dependent on you instead of you being dependent on them for life and breath and ransom and everything. What pleases God is when He is shown to be the giver in our service of Him. If we serve God as though we are the giver and He is the needy one, He is not pleased. It makes Him look needy and dependent. But He's not.

So verse 18 says, "Whoever thus serves Christ is acceptable to God and approved by men." That is, whoever serves Christ — obeys Christ, pursues the righteousness that He commands — in the way described in verse 17 is pleasing to God. Namely, the one who depends on the Holy Spirit for what he pursues. The one who serves with the deep and happy confidence that God is always serving us in our service of Him. He always remains the supplier. Always.

The text that we pray more than any other in our service of Christ at Bethlehem Church is probably 1 Peter 4:11. Peter exhorts each of us to be "one who serves by the strength that God supplies — in order that in everything God may be glorified through Jesus Christ." Serve with the expectation that the strength to serve will come from God. Then God will get all the glory. Do you want your serving to be an expression of His kingdom or of your power?

What pleases God, and wins the serious approval of others, is when our serving is the fruit of the Holy Spirit. This is why the writer to the Hebrews closed his book with this benediction, "Now may the God of peace . . . equip you with everything good that you may do His will, working in us that which is pleasing in His sight, through Jesus Christ, to whom be glory forever and ever. Amen." God works in us what is pleasing in His sight. And the fact that He works it in us is part of what makes it pleasing in His sight.

The kingdom of God is not food and drink. It is righteousness, peace, and joy which come by the powerful working of the Holy Spirit in our lives. The one who serves Christ in this way — depending on the work of the Spirit for all the help you need and renouncing all self-reliance — pleases God and manifests His kingdom in the church and extends His kingdom in the world.

So then, Bethlehem Church, as verse 19 says, "Let us pursue what makes for peace and for mutual upbuilding." Don't flaunt your freedom. Love your brothers and sisters. And do it not in your own strength, but in the Holy Spirit. This is the kingdom of God. This is His rule in our midst."[18]

---

[18] Sermon by Pastor John Piper www.desiringgod.org Copyright 2005 John Piper. Used by permission.

THE AGE TO COME

SIN BROKEN / MANKIND AND GOD RESTORED

The Pure in Heart will see God

"Blessed are the pure in heart, for they shall see God" (Mt. 5:8).

Enter into Joy

"His master said to him, 'Well done, good and faithful slave. You were faithful with a few things, I will put you in charge of many things; enter into the joy of your master'" (Mt. 25:21).

The Grain is Gathered

"Allow both to grow together until the harvest; and in the time of the harvest I will say to the reapers, 'First gather up the tares and bind them in bundles to burn them up; but gather the wheat into my barn'" (Mt. 13:30). "But He said, 'No; for while you are gathering up the tares, you may uproot the wheat with them" (Mt. 13:29). "But when the crop permits, He immediately puts in the sickle, because the harvest has come" (Mk. 4:29). "His winnowing fork is in His hand, and He will thoroughly clear His threshing floor; and He will gather His wheat into the barn, but He will burn up the chaff with unquenchable fire" (Mt. 3:12). "And another angel came out of the temple, crying out with a loud voice to Him who sat on the cloud, 'Put in your sickle and reap, for the hour to reap has come, because the harvest of the earth is ripe'" (Rev. 14:15).

The Sheep Separated

"He will put the sheep on His right and the goats on the left" (Mt. 25:33).

Drinking the Cup Anew in the Father's Kingdom

"Truly I say to you, I will never again drink of the fruit of the vine until that day when I drink it new in the kingdom of God" (Mk. 14:25).

Eating and Drinking at Jesus' Table

"You may eat and drink at My table in My kingdom, and you will sit on thrones judging the twelve tribes of Israel" (Lk. 22:30).

Wedding Feast

"Jesus spoke to them again in parables, saying, "The kingdom of heaven may be compared to a king who gave a wedding feast for his son. And he sent out his slaves to call those who had been invited to the wedding feast, and they were unwilling to come. Again he sent out other slaves saying, 'Tell those who have been invited, "Behold, I have prepared my dinner; my oxen and my fattened livestock are all butchered and everything is ready; come to the wedding feast.'" But they paid no attention and went their way, one to his own farm, another to his business, and the rest seized his slaves and mistreated them and killed them. But the king was enraged, and he sent his armies and destroyed those murderers and set their city on fire. Then he said to his slaves, 'The wedding is ready, but those who were invited were not worthy. Go therefore to the main highways, and as many as you find there, invite to the wedding feast.' Those slaves went out into the streets and gathered together all they found, both evil and good; and the wedding hall was filled with dinner guests. But when the king came in to look over the dinner guests, he saw a man there who was not dressed in wedding clothes, and he said to him, 'Friend, how did you come in here without wedding clothes?' And the man was speechless. Then the king said to the servants, 'Bind him hand and foot, and throw him into the outer darkness; in that place there will be weeping and gnashing of teeth.' For many are called, but few are chosen" (Mt. 22:1-14). "Then the kingdom of heaven will be comparable to ten virgins, who took their lamps and went out to meet the bridegroom. Five of them were foolish, and five were prudent. For when the foolish took their lamps, they took no oil with them, but the prudent took oil in flasks along with their lamps. Now while the bridegroom was delaying, they all got drowsy and began to sleep. But at midnight there was a shout, 'Behold, the bridegroom! Come out to meet him.' Then all those virgins rose and trimmed their lamps. The foolish said to the prudent, 'Give us some of your oil, for our lamps are going out.' But the prudent answered, 'No, there will not be enough for us and you too; go instead to the dealers and buy some for yourselves.' And while they were going away to make the purchase, the bridegroom came, and those who were ready went in with him to the wedding feast; and the door was shut. Later the other virgins also came, saying, 'Lord, lord, open up for us.' But He answered, 'Truly I say to you, I do not know you'" (Mt. 25:1-12).

The Banquet

"I say to you that many will come from east and west, and recline at the table with Abraham, Isaac and Jacob in the kingdom of heaven" (Mt. 8:11). "But He said to him, 'A man was giving a big dinner, and he invited many'" (Lk. 14:16).

THE EYE OF A NEEDLE

Do you want to recline at the table with King Jesus in heaven? I am sure that you do. That's why it's important to share with you who the Bible says will not. Let's look at the book of Mark. It records: "It is easier for a camel to go through the eye of a needle than for a rich man to enter the kingdom of God" (Mk. 10:25).

The demon spirit of greed has a demonic stronghold on many. And I am not just talking about the individuals in Hollywood that are seeking fame and fortune; I'm talking about individuals sitting in the church. If you are not honoring God in your finances, you are in rebellion and there is a curse on your life. It is that simple. How do I know? Because God stated it in four thousand million Christian Bibles, that's how I know. Being a minister of the gospel, I want to make sure you know. What you do is not my concern. My job is just to inform you.

Let's look at the story of the rich young ruler. "As He was setting out on a journey, a man ran up to Him and knelt before Him, and asked Him, 'Good Teacher, what shall I do to inherit eternal life?' And Jesus said to him, 'Why do you call Me good? No one is good except God alone. You know the commandments, "DO NOT MURDER, DO NOT COMMIT ADULTERY, DO NOT STEAL, DO NOT BEAR FALSE WITNESS, DO NOT DEFRAUD, HONOR YOUR FATHER AND

MOTHER.'" And he said to Him, 'Teacher, I have kept all these things from my youth up.' Looking at him, Jesus felt a love for him and said to him, 'One thing you lack: go and sell all you possess and give to the poor, and you will have treasure in heaven; and come, follow Me.' But at these words he was saddened, and he went away grieving, for he was one who owned much property. And Jesus, looking around, said to His disciples, 'How hard it will be for those who are wealthy to enter the kingdom of God'" (Mr. 10:17-23)!

Now I want you to understand something. That does not mean that Jesus wants everyone to sell everything they have and give it to the poor. The rich young ruler's heart was wrapped around money. Jesus knows everything that is in our hearts, good and bad.

Did Jesus chase after the grieving man and say: "Wait a minute. You don't have to sell everything. I'll tell you what. Just sell fifty percent and sow some money into my ministry"? No He didn't. Can you imagine the opportunity that man missed? He could have sowed money and helped Jesus with the works of God. So, let me ask you a question. Do you think the rich young ruler is spending eternity with God?

One of the main purposes in writing this book is to increase the reader's heavenly perspective. Most individuals can imagine three, five, some even ten years. Can you imagine four thousand million years? No you cannot. Four thousand million years is like a drop in a bucket compared to all the oceans on planet earth. I am talking about forever and ever and ever. With that heavenly perspective, how important is money?

I heard Sister Paula White state on television that "The Holy Bible is a book of revelation." It lets us know where our heart is. She went on to say that our checkbook is a book of revelation and that by looking at our checkbooks we can tell where our heart is. In order to have an intimate relationship with the Lord, we must put the kingdom of God before our finances.

Chapter 11

INTIMACY EQUALS FAVOR

Humility, obedience, faith and a very intimate relationship with God will produce much favor with Him. The two key scriptures that I will be expounding on are: "And God is able to make all grace abound to you, so that always having all sufficiency in everything you may have an abundance for every good deed" (2 Cor. 9:8) and "But seek first His kingdom and His righteousness, and all these things will be added to you" (Mt. 6:33). It's vital to seek His face and not His hand. Some may seek first His kingdom but not His righteousness. Seeking His righteousness is the major key to having favor with God.

The first scripture states: "God is able." He is only able if we let Him. Jesus' brother James said: "Draw near to God and He will draw near to you" (Jas. 4:8). I don't believe God will force His blessings on anyone, do you? Well Saul on the road to Damascus was a close call. Anyway, that scripture goes on to say: "having all sufficiency in everything." Can I break it down for you? The word sufficiency in the Greek means: "a perfect condition of life in which no aid or support is needed/sufficiency of the necessities of life/a mind contented with its lot, contentment."[19]

---

[19] Online Bible North America Software (Strong's Numbers)

I am entering into a new season in my walk with Almighty God, creator of heaven and earth. When a saint enters a new season, many material things are needed that were not required for the last seasons. Wherever I go, everything I have needed happens to be on sale. I was looking to buy an office chair for two years. When I finally found one that met my needs, I asked the gentleman in Office Depot how often they go on sale. He said, "Rarely." I informed him the Lord would have it for sale the following week. The following week I went to pick it up. It was $129 marked down from $199.

I went in to see this same salesman again last Friday and informed him I needed a portable printer to prepare my sermons when I was out in the villages in Mexico. The printer was $299 and he informed me they just about never go on sale. I informed him I would be in the following week; that the Lord was taking care of it, because I had favor with God. The following week it was on sale for $249. I knew for two years I would need those items. I didn't seek the items. I sought God and then He sent me for them when favor was involved.

When we are diligent with the things of God and stay focused on the kingdom of God, then everything else will be added. The Bible says: "Poor is he who works with a negligent hand, but the hand of the diligent makes rich" (Pr. 10:4). God will always bless the righteous that are diligent. That's why I love the following verses: "But let all those that put their trust in thee rejoice: let them ever shout for joy, because thou defendest them: let them also that love thy name be joyful in thee. For thou, Lord, wilt bless the righteous; with favour wilt thou compass him as with a shield. (Ps. 5:11,12 KJV). "Fools make a mock at sin: but among the righteous there is favour" (Pr. 14:9 KJV). "For You are the glory of their strength, and by Your favor our horn is exalted" (Ps. 89:17).

Some Benefits of God's Favor

1. Promotion - "But the Lord was with Joseph, and shewed him mercy, and gave him favour in the sight of the keeper of the prison" (Gen. 39:21, KJV).

2. Restoration - "And I will give this people favour in the sight of the Egyptians: and it shall come to pass, that, when ye go, ye shall not go empty" (Ex. 3:21, KJV).

3. Respect - "And the Lord gave the people favour in the sight of the Egyptians. Moreover the man Moses was very great in the land of Egypt, in the sight of Pharaoh's servants, and in the sight of the people" (Ex. 11:3, KJV).

4. Material Blessings - "And of Naphtali he said, 'O Naphtali, satisfied with favour, and full with the blessing of the Lord: possess thou the west and the south'" (Deut. 33:23, KJV).

5. Victory - "For it was of the Lord to harden their hearts, that they should come against Israel in battle, that He might destroy them utterly, and that they might have no favour, but that He might destroy them, as the Lord commanded Moses" (Jos. 11:20, KJV).

6. Acknowledgment - "And Saul sent to Jesse, saying, 'Let David, I pray thee, stand before me; for he hath found favour in My sight'" (1 Sam. 16:22, KJV).

7. Special Treatment - "And the king loved Esther above all the women, and she obtained grace and favour in his sight more than all the virgins; so that he set the royal crown upon her head, and made her queen instead of Vashti" (Est. 2:17, KJV).

God's Back versus God's Face

Jeremiah 18:17 reads, "Like a wind from the east, I will scatter them before their enemies; I will show them My back and not My face in the day of their disaster." The Hebrew definition for the word "scatter" means "to dash in pieces."

The Lord says, "I will show them My back and not My face." This is not good news. This tends to create immeasurable hardship. We learn from the book of Numbers that His "face" indicates His favor. Those scriptures state, "Speak to Aaron and to his sons, saying, 'Thus you shall bless the sons of Israel. You shall say to them: "The Lord bless you, and keep you; the Lord make His face shine on you, and be gracious to you. The Lord lift up His countenance on you, and give you peace."' So they shall invoke My name on the sons of Israel, and I then will bless them" (Num. 6:23-27).

Setting Priorities

I hope this chapter has challenged you. I find in my Christian walk that setting my priorities, especially the managing of time, is a key component to a life finding favor with God. I am a steward of money, talents and time. I must be very careful of distractions. I must set my mind and be about my Fathers business, taking great care not to waver.

I would like to leave you with what I consider the most powerful scriptures in the entire Bible regarding favor: "And the angel came in unto her, and said, 'Hail, thou that art highly favoured, the Lord is with thee: blessed art thou among women.' And when she saw him, she was troubled at his saying, and cast in her mind what manner of salutation this should be. And the angel said unto her, 'Fear not, Mary: for thou hast found favour with God'" (Lk. 1:28-30 KJV).

SET YOUR MIND

Colossians 3:2

We have studied a great deal of astonishing information in this compilation. I hope and pray it was and is a blessing for you. Hopefully, by now you have a deeper and clearer understanding regarding the kingdom of God, Christ' suffering and death, along with a vast array of other vital information for your walk with the Lord Jesus.

I also pray and hope this material has increased your heavenly perspective. The following verse is a major key to pressing toward the prize: "Set your mind on the things above, not on the things that are on earth" (Col. 3:2). The word "set" in this verse is critical for me. In the Greek it means: "to seek, to strive for/to seek one's interest or advantage."[20]

Let's look at some other verses that are a blessing: "Finally, brethren, whatever is true, whatever is honorable, whatever is right, whatever is pure, whatever is lovely, whatever is of good repute, if there is any excellence and if anything worthy of praise, dwell on these things" (Php. 4:8); "Therefore humble your-selves under the mighty hand of God, that He may exalt you at the proper time, casting all your anxiety on Him, because He cares for you"

---

[20] Online Bible North America Software (Strong's Numbers)

(1 Pet. 5:6-7); "Be careful for nothing..." (Php. 4:6 KJV). Set your mind on the kingdom of God and His righteousness.

MY OTHER PUBLICATIONS

To inquire about other books written by Eugene Carvalho, please visit the website below.

WWW.NEWWINEMISSIONS.INFO

<u>NOTES</u>

NOTES

<u>NOTES</u>

NOTES

<u>NOTES</u>

Made in the USA
Charleston, SC
03 October 2010